Sti

Poo-ems

Ta-doo!

written & illustrated
by Jason L. Witter

Stinky Monster Poo-ems

Printed in the United States of America.

ISBN-13: 978-1729526668
ISBN-10: 1729526667

First Edition: September 2018

witterworks1@gmail.com
www.facebook.com/witterworks
Instagram: @tiniest_vampire
www.witterworks.com

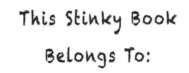

This Stinky Book

Belongs To:

_____

And now
for
some
STINKY
POO-EMS!

RUDE

Why does this llamacorn
look so grumpy
& poopy-hearted?
Well, the truth of
the matter is...
somebody
just farted.

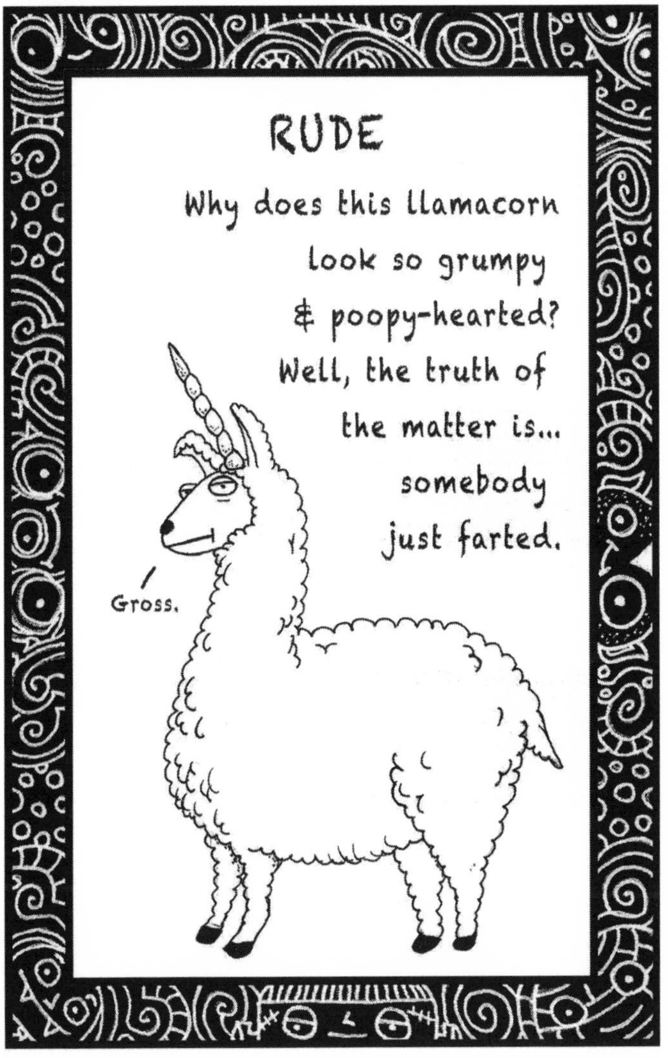
Gross.

Werewolf Droppings

There's a werewolf
in the cupboard.
He used to live
under the sink.
But he pooped there
so much,
it really started
to stink.

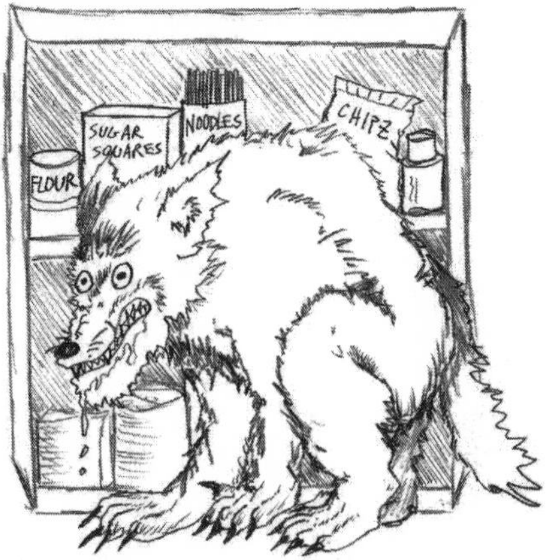
SUGAR SQUARES
NOODLES
CHIPZ
FLOUR

He tried to blame the children,
but we knew they had been framed.
Now he hides in the pantry,
feeling lonely and ashamed.
So, here is the lesson,
if you want to save face,
when it comes to poopin',
make sure you go
in the right place!

Pigeonzilla!

When Pigeonzilla came to town,
he knocked
every single building down.
With him came horror,
terror,
unspeakable dread!
But really,
the worst
part is...
he took a poo
on each
& every
person's
perplexed
head.

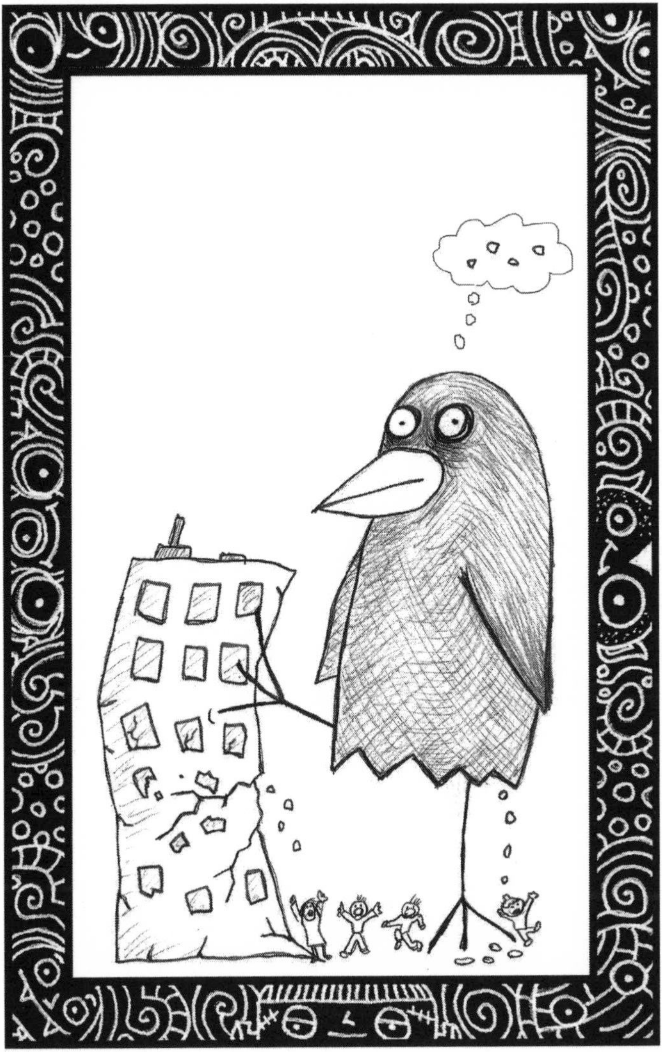

Raisin Pie

Raisin Pie,

Raisin Pie,

Tastes kind of strange...

...I wonder why.

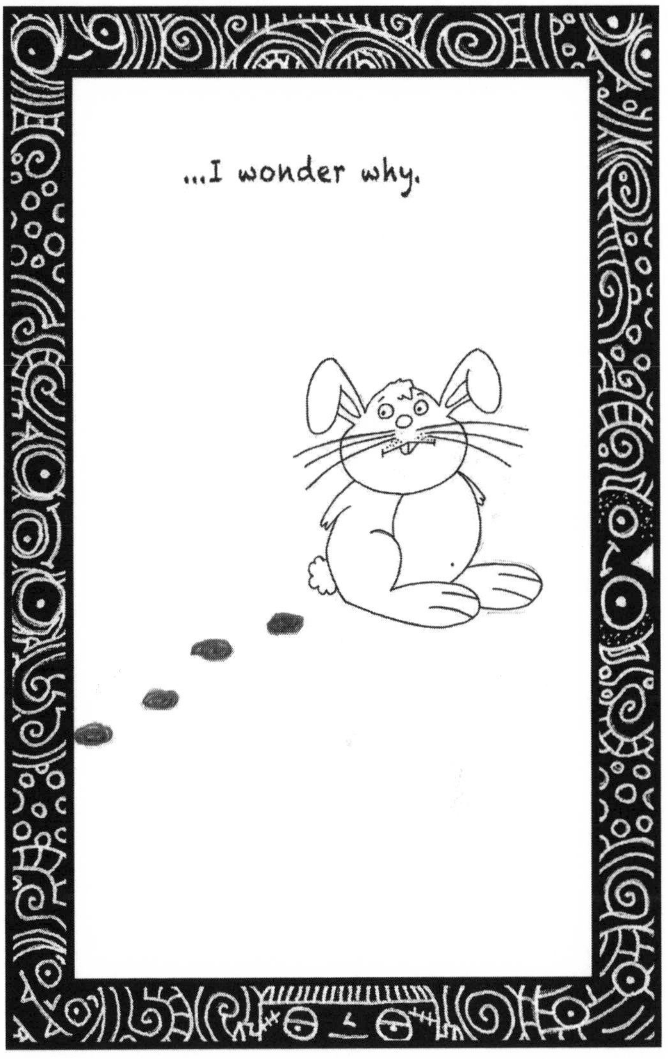

Always Be Prepared

One dark
and stormy night,
the mummy ran out
of toilet tissue!
It gave him
such a fright!
Okay... it really wasn't
that big of an issue.

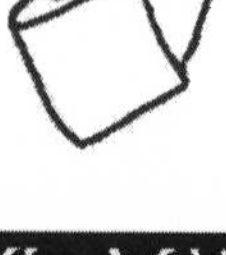

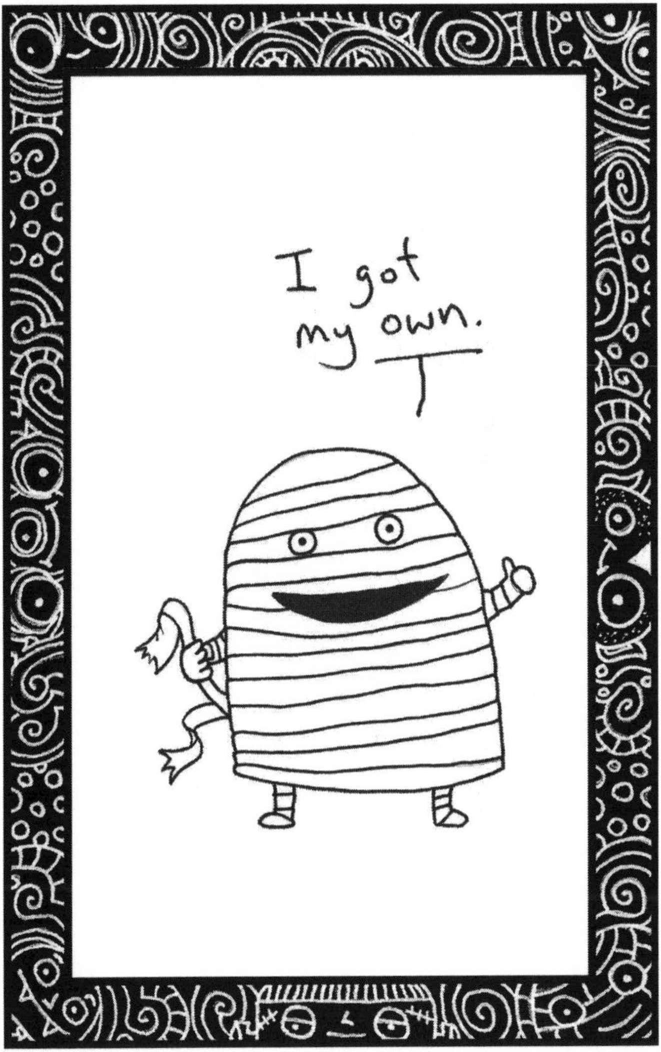
I got my own.

Watch Your Step

When Big Foot
came to town,
he wanted
to trick or treat.
The only problem was
he crushed
everybody
with his feet!
This would
have been okay,
a good time
could still be had,
if only
his big ol' feet
didn't smell
so big ol' bad!

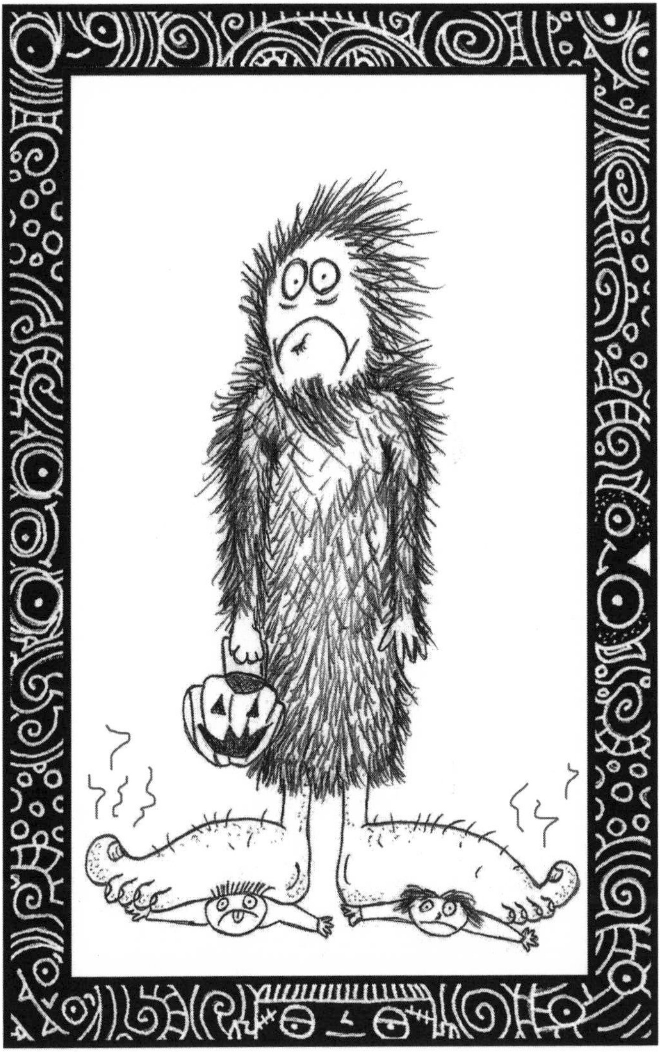

Free Thinker, Free Stinker

After seeing a

motivational speaker,

Jonathan Whiskers MacSocks

decided to become

an inspirational seeker

by thinking

outside of the box!

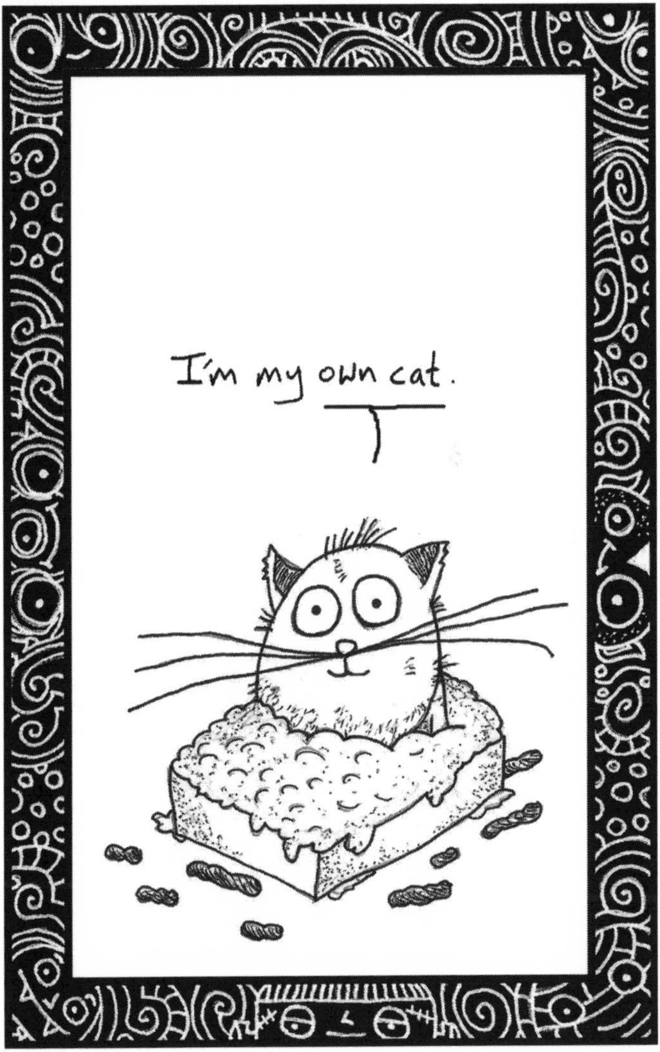
I'm my own cat.

Ol' Booger Brain

When you throw out your umbrella

'cause it's starting to rain,

and you're the silly fella

putting putty down the drain,

and you stop to look around

in front of an oncoming train,

you plant pennies in the ground

hoping dollars you'll obtain...

when you do all of these things

with no knowledge ever gained,

then you're the ding-a-ling

who's got boogers on the brain!

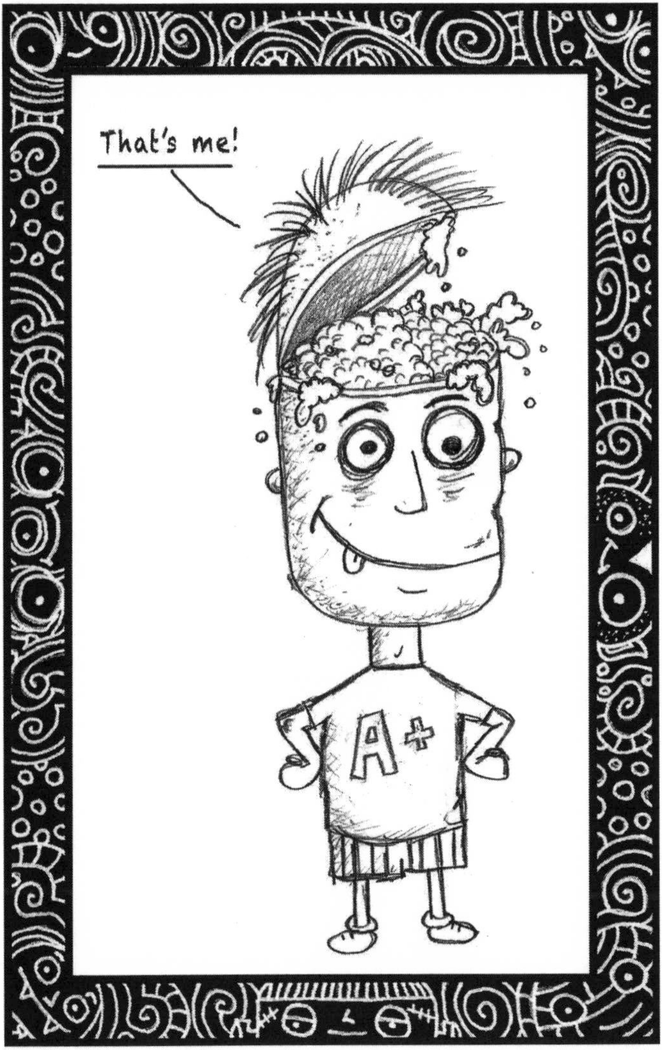
That's me!

Stuck

The swamp monster

awoke

with great plans

for the day.

But when he got stuck

in the toilet,

they were all

flushed away.

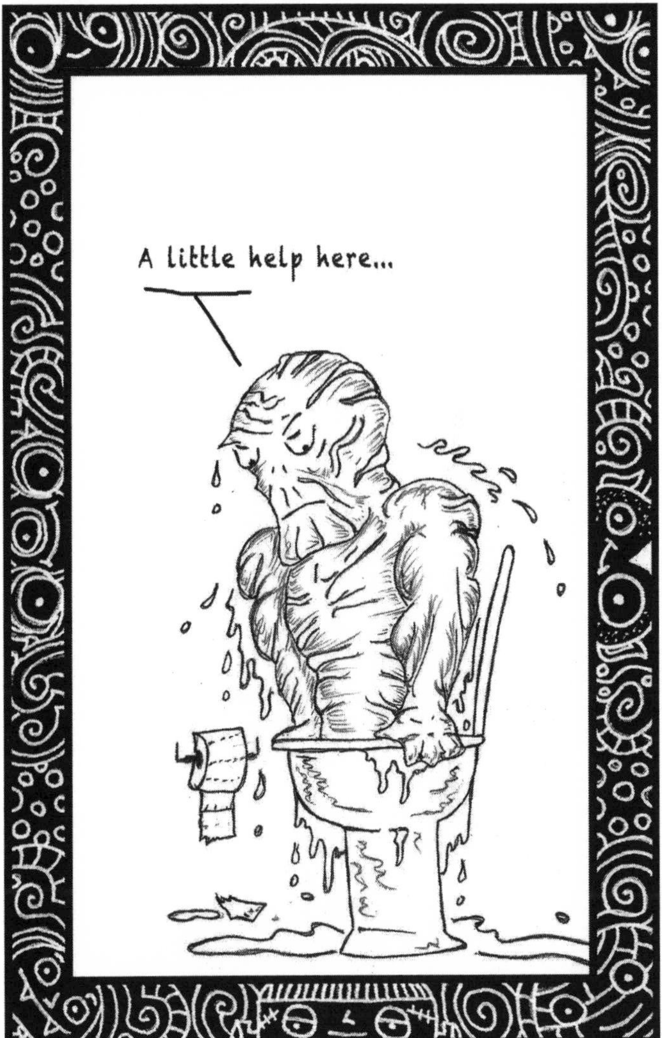
A little help here...

So Stinky!

Here's a cute
little puff,
I'm sure you'll want to
pet him and stuff.
But though he looks
adorable,
he actually smells
quite horrible.
You should really run
and make it on the double,
cuz those circles above him
are a bunch of fart bubbles!

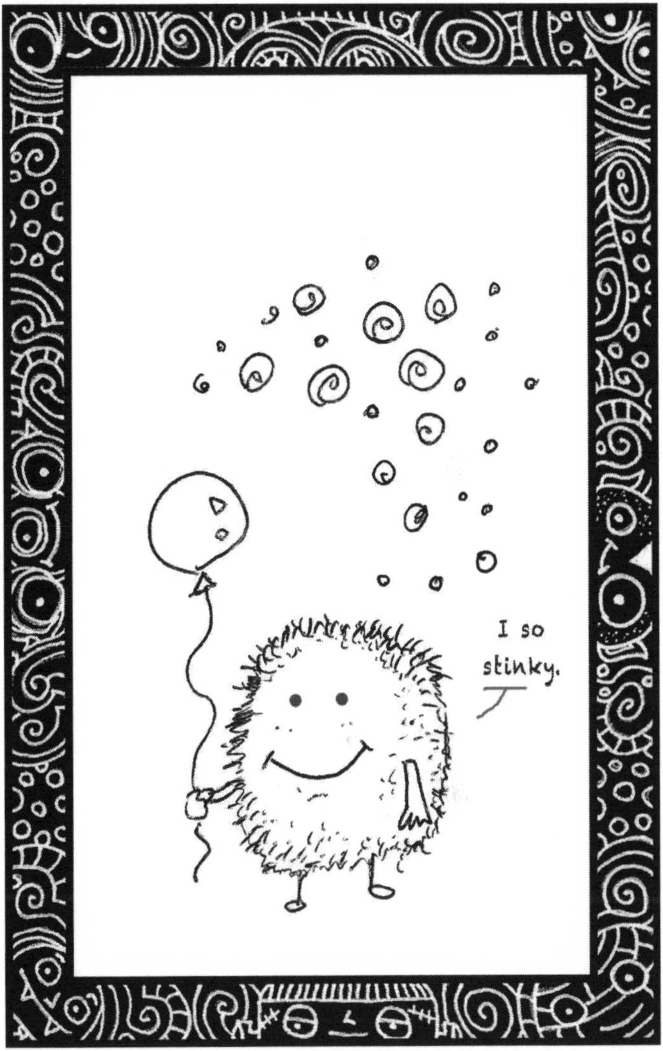
I so stinky.

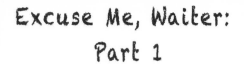

Excuse Me, Waiter: Part 1

There's a finger in my stew,
oh, a finger in my stew!
How it got there,
I haven't got a clue!
I thought it was a carrot,
oh, I thought it was a carrot!
But now I don't want
to even go near it!
I'd like to eat, you see,
oh, I'd like to eat, you see?
But it's kind of hard to eat
when my dinner keeps
pointing at me!!!

Excuse Me, Waiter: Part 2

There's a toe in my soup,

oh, a toe in my soup!

Why in the world

is there a toe in my soup?

There's a toe in my soup,

oh, a toe in my soup!

Well, I guess it's better

than a big ol' pile of poop!

Here's a little ditty
'bout Jack and Diane,
two crazy kids
who like to eat Spam.
One slice for breakfast
with jelly or jam,
and funky French toast
smothered in Spam.
When lunch rolls 'round,
no turkey or ham,
just a sweet stack
of delicious fried Spam.
What's for dinner?
Here's candied yam,
mushy green peas
and a huge side of Spam.
A midnight snack?
That would be grand!
Cookies & milk?
Forget that... bring out the Spam!!!

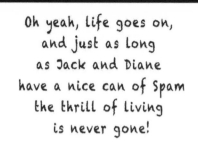

Oh yeah, life goes on,
and just as long
as Jack and Diane
have a nice can of Spam
the thrill of living
is never gone!

Spam Song

Franken-Poo

(or The Modern Poo-Metheus)

Dr. Frank did not want
the world's waste
to go to waste,
so he made a plan
and got to it
with great haste.
He went
to the sewers,
he knew
just what to do,
he filled up
a great, big bucket
& he made a
Franken-poo!

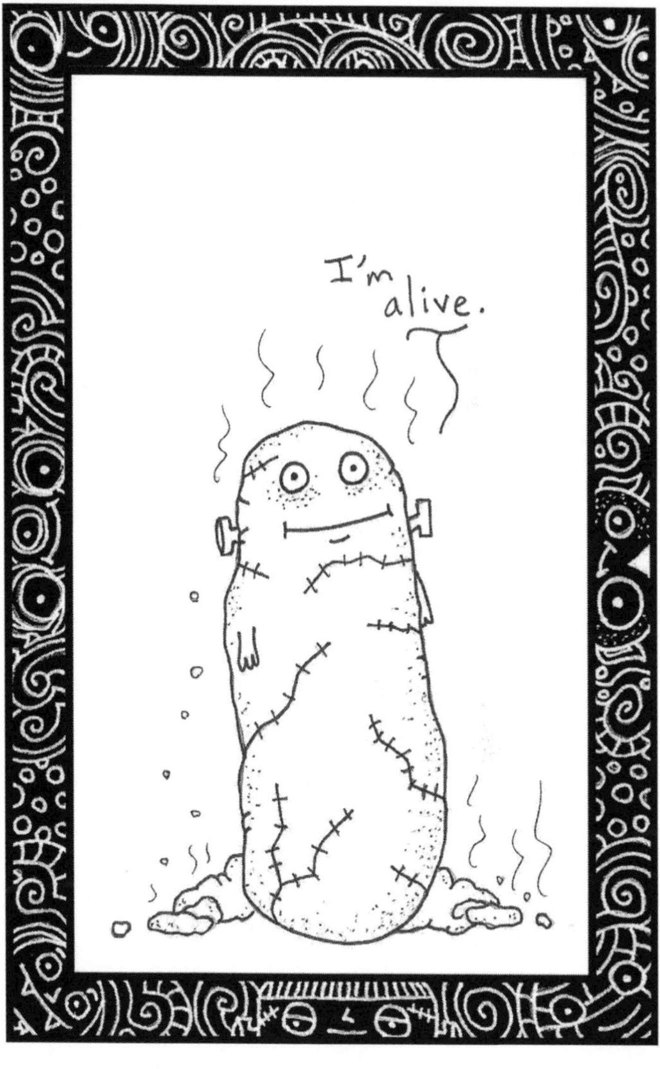
I'm alive.

Tater Man

Tater Man, Tater Man,

does whatever

a tater can.

Tater goo, tater poo,

what exactly

does a tater do?

Not much.

T

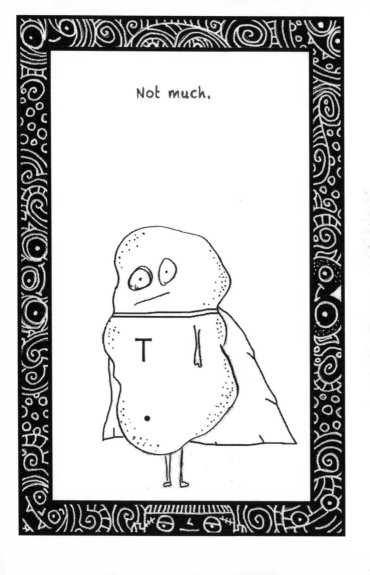

Bad Decisions

This cat
was going to
hand out
all of
the candy
to all
of the kids
on All Hallows' Eve.
Instead...
he ate
all of the candy.
Then...
he ate
all of the kids.
Now...

... he is
just going to heave.

I can't believe I ate the whole thing.

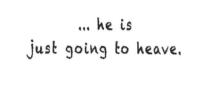

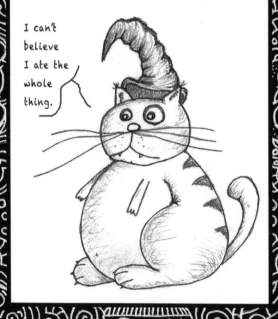

Look Out Below!

Cap'n Hook was troubled
by an itch upon his butt.
So, he went to scratch it.
Now, you might say, "so what?"
But here is the problem,
just between you and me,
he used the wrong "hand"
now it's a full moon at sea!

Oops.

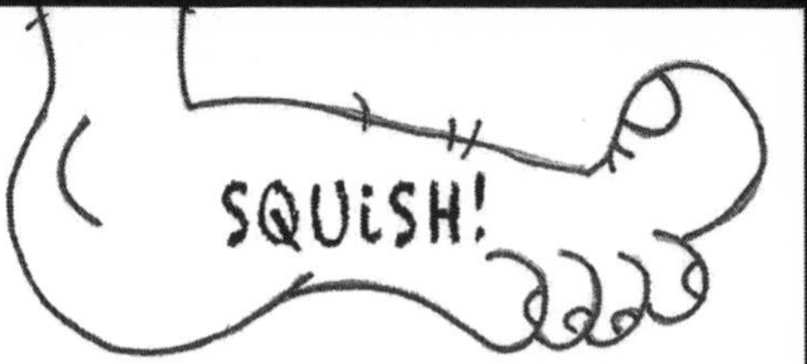
SQUiSH!

When we go to sleep
and turn in for the night,
we tell one another,
"Don't let the bed bugs bite."
When the bed bugs go to sleep,
I wonder what they do,
maybe say to each other,
"Don't let the humans squash you!"

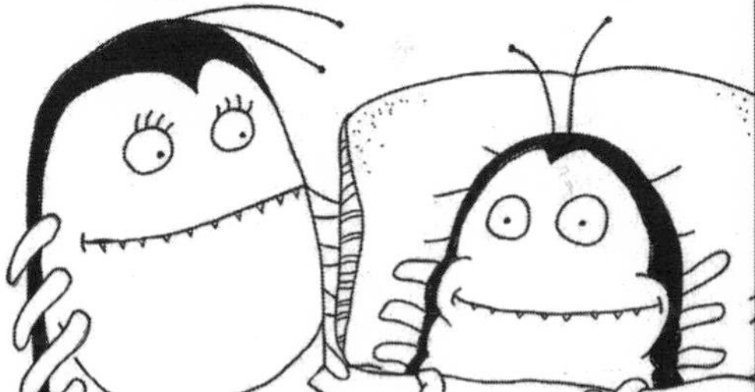

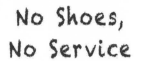

No Shoes,
No Service

When it came time
to get married,
the Froggs
had the blues...
They'd gotten
all dressed up,
but forgot
to put on their shoes!

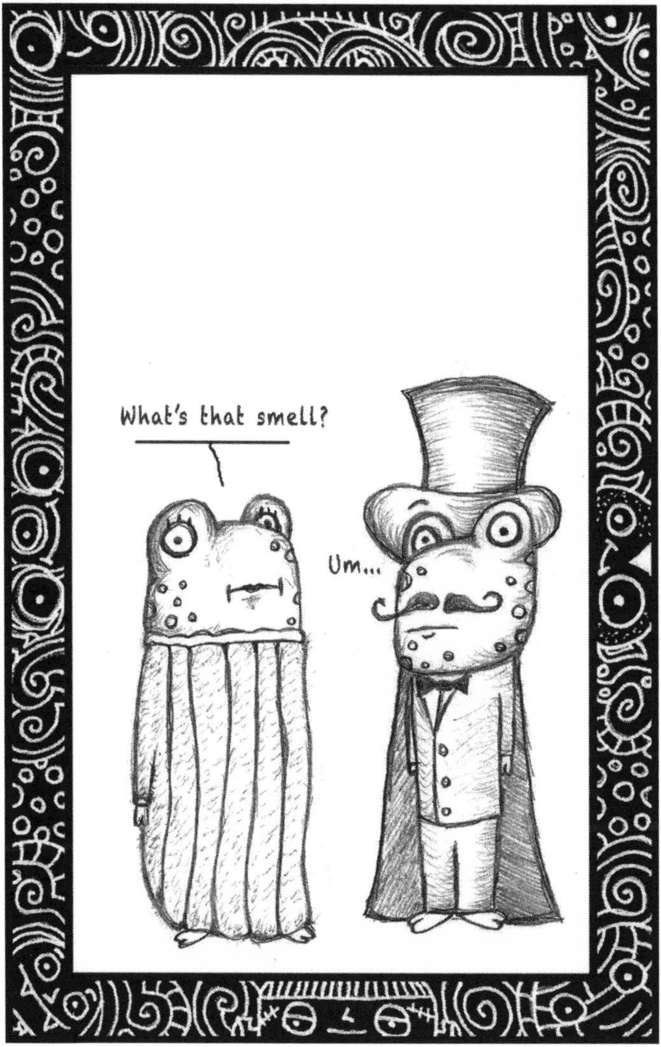
What's that smell?
Um...

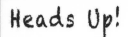

Heads Up!

Have you met the gorilla
with the umbrella?
Well, I'll bet
he's a really plum fella!
And if you're polite to him,
he'll be kind to you,
but if your manners are slim,
watch out for flung poo!!!

DO NOT ANNOY THE GORILLA!

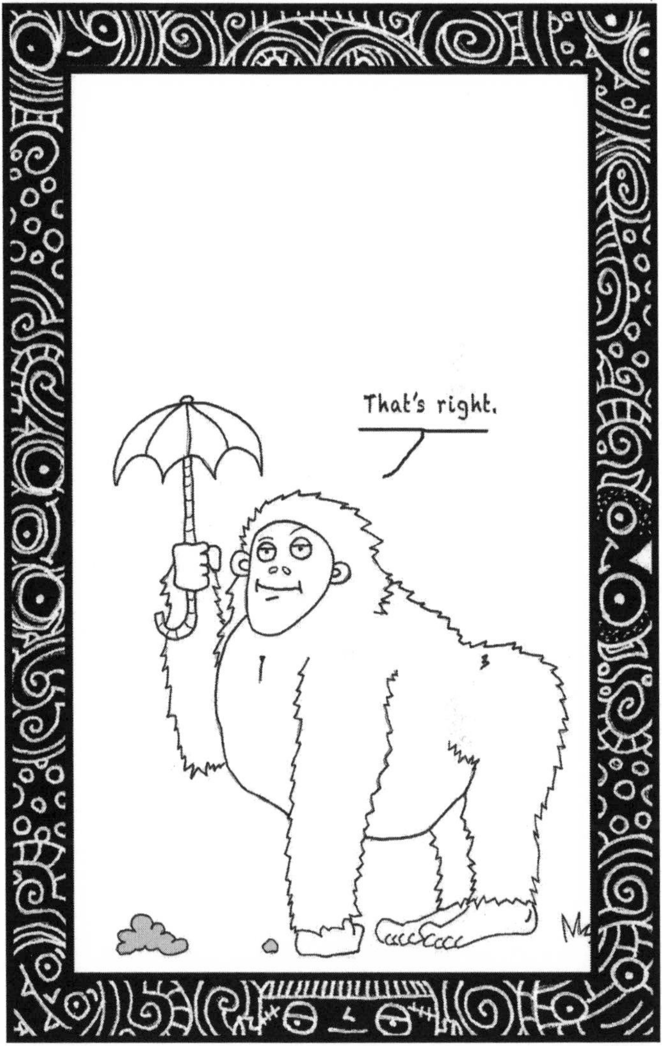
That's right.

Hospital Food

What's that awful smell?

I can taste it

in my ears!

Oh.

It's just

the vampire nurse...

she's been dead

for a hundred years!

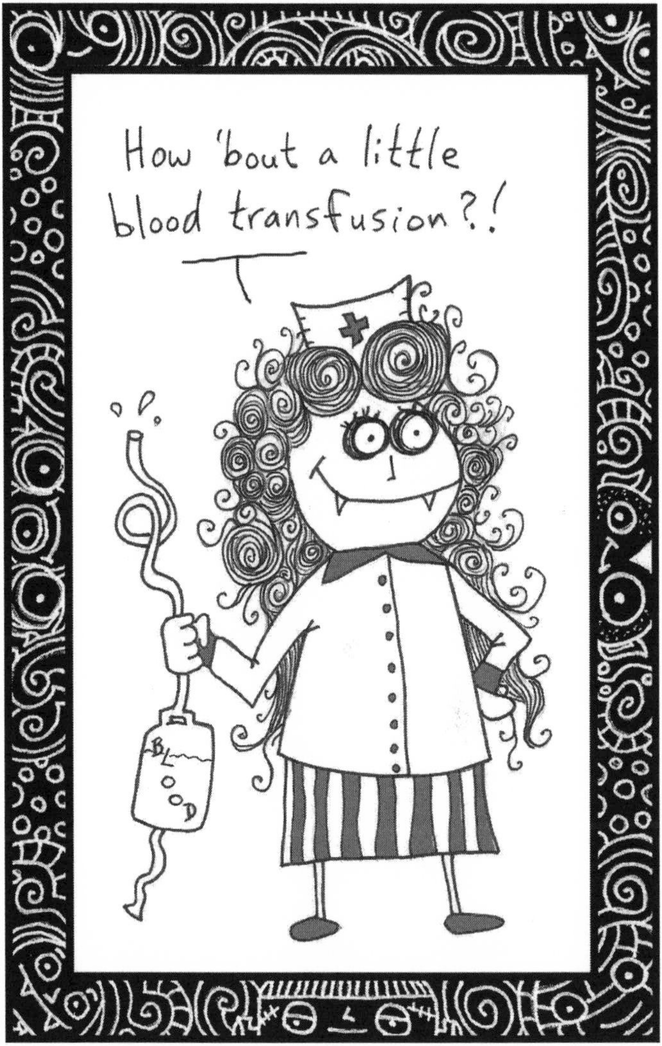
How 'bout a little blood transfusion?!
BLOOD

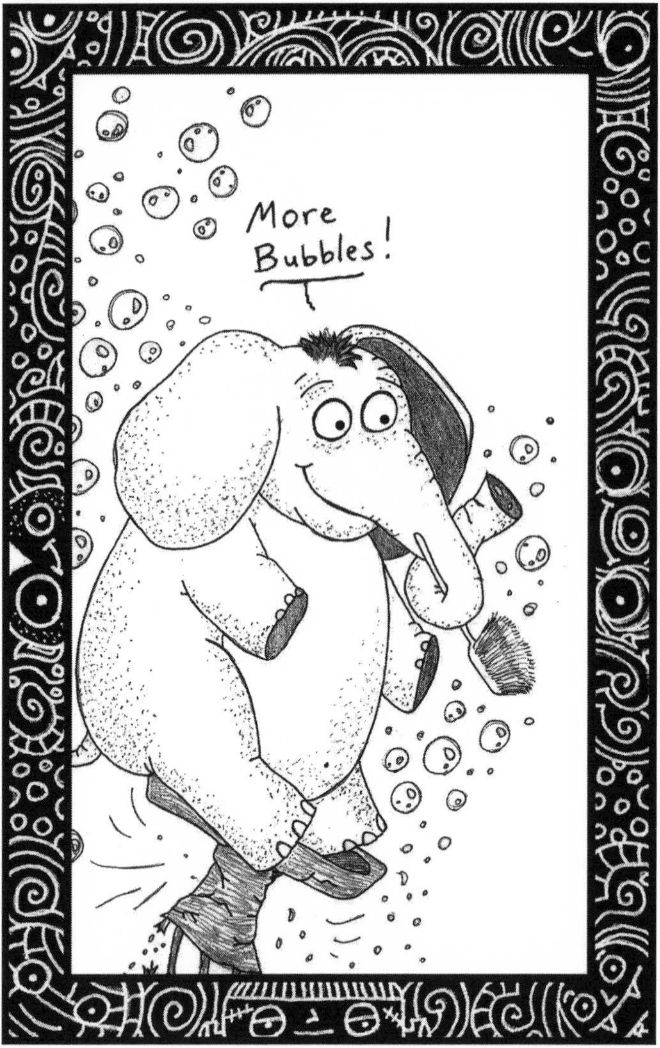
More Bubbles!

Pachydermatology

Everyone should know
(at least one would think)
it's foolish
to give an elephant
a bath
in the sink.

ZOMBIE POO

(or Poo-Pocalypse Now!)

Something is happening!

Causing terror and strife!

The doo-doo in the sewers

is coming to life!!!

It's attacking at will,

and this is the scoop,

the end is near...

all because of our poop!

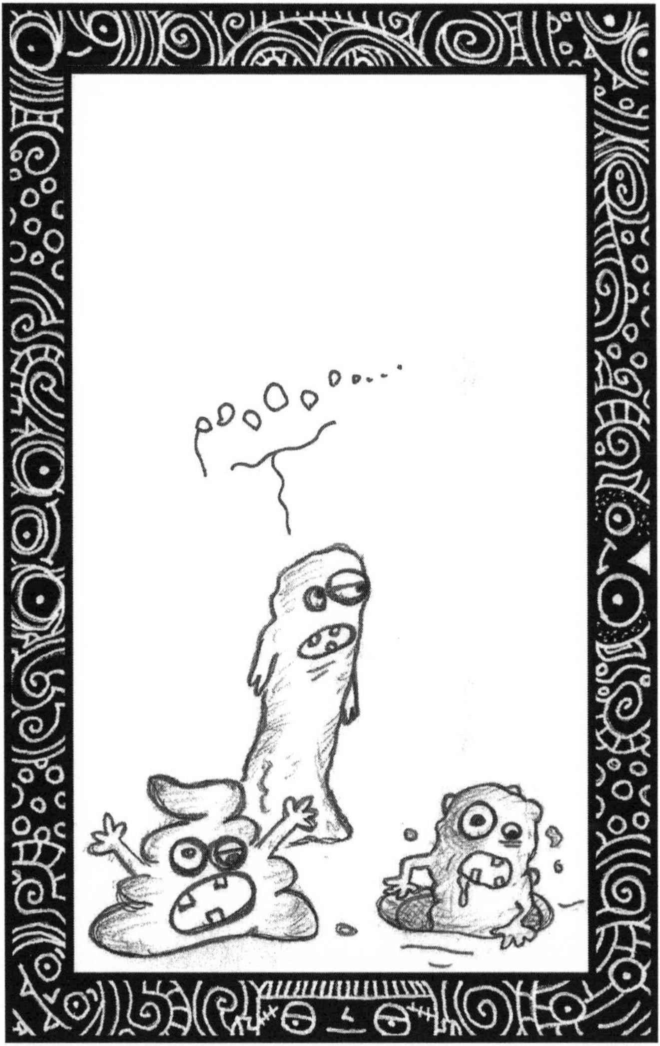

Muddy Larry

Bloody Mary! Bloody Mary!
Bloody Mary!
Say it three times,
and you'll see something scary!
Watch her morbid image
appear in the mirror,
filling all the children
with loads and loads of fear!
But even Bloody Mary
needs to take a vacation.
So, she asks her brother Larry
to fill in for her station.
Muddy Larry! Muddy Larry!
Muddy Larry!
Say it three times,
and it won't be very scary...

... but you'll probably have to grab
the mop and the broom,
and spend a few hours
cleaning up the bathroom!

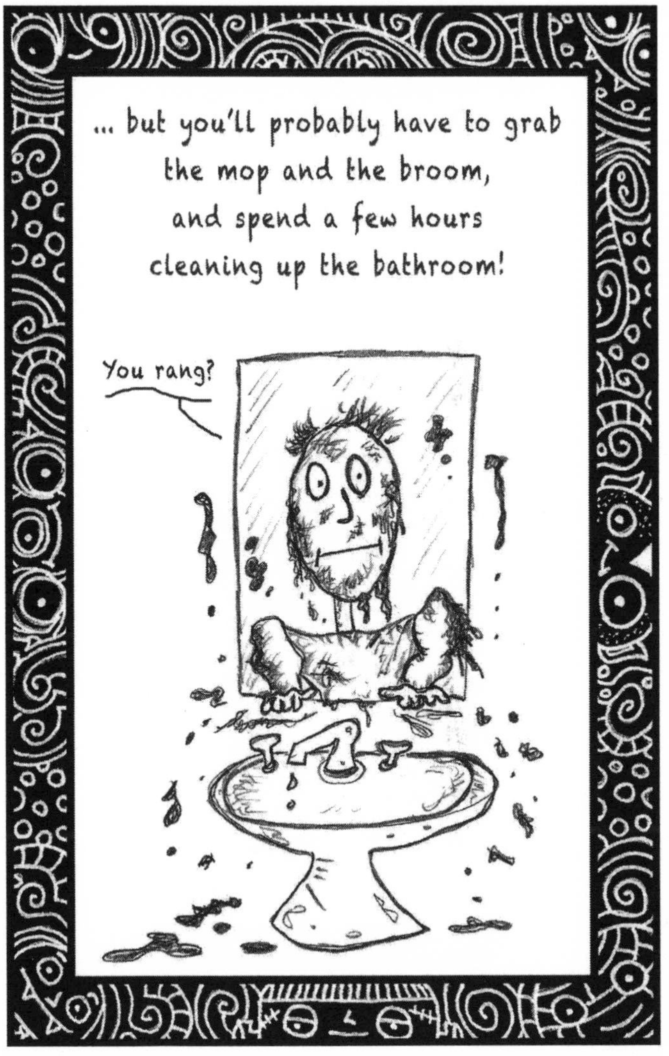
You rang?

Foot Storm

I don't like feet.
They are gross,
to say the most,
and they stink
like rotten meat.
I don't like feet.
They get so smelly,
upset my belly,
they can
take a back seat.
I don't like feet.
Open toed shoes,
give me the blues,
return 'em,
here's the receipt.
I don't like feet.

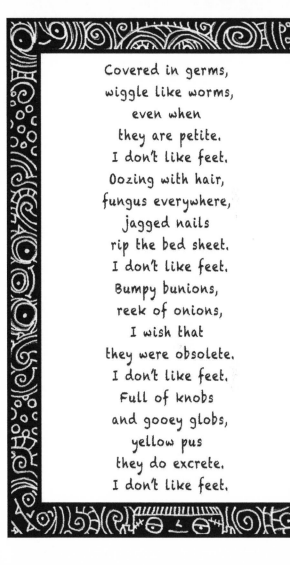

Covered in germs,
wiggle like worms,
even when
they are petite.
I don't like feet.
Oozing with hair,
fungus everywhere,
jagged nails
rip the bed sheet.
I don't like feet.
Bumpy bunions,
reek of onions,
I wish that
they were obsolete.
I don't like feet.
Full of knobs
and gooey globs,
yellow pus
they do excrete.
I don't like feet.

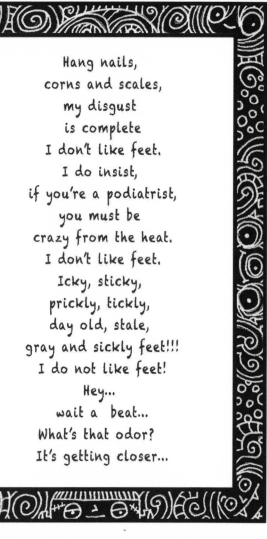

Hang nails,
corns and scales,
my disgust
is complete
I don't like feet.
I do insist,
if you're a podiatrist,
you must be
crazy from the heat.
I don't like feet.
Icky, sticky,
prickly, tickly,
day old, stale,
gray and sickly feet!!!
I do not like feet!
Hey...
wait a beat...
What's that odor?
It's getting closer...

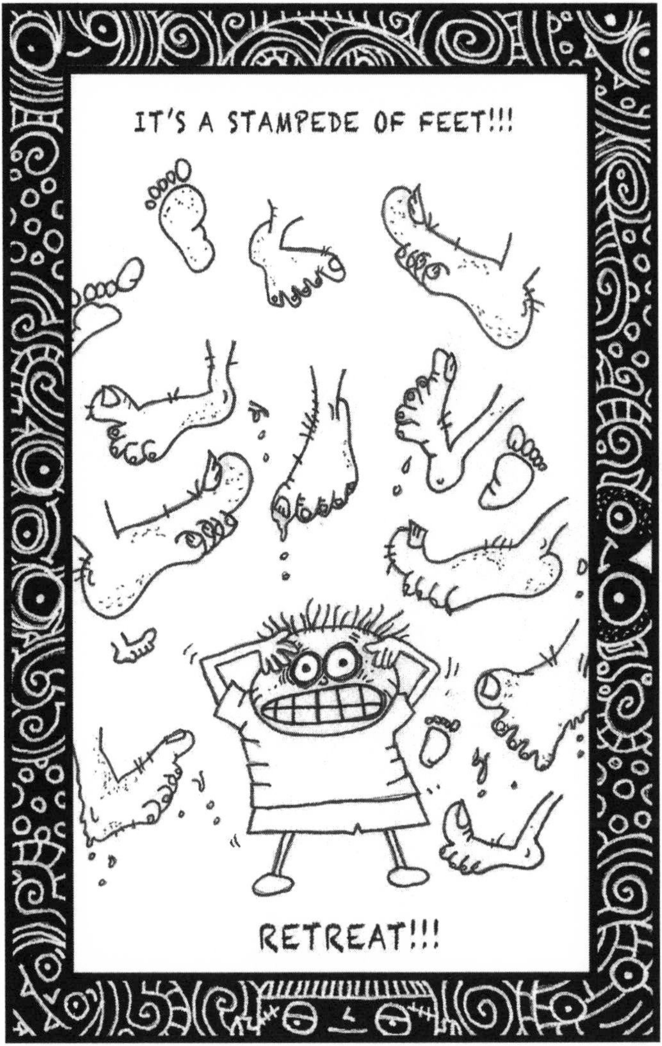
IT'S A STAMPEDE OF FEET!!!
RETREAT!!!

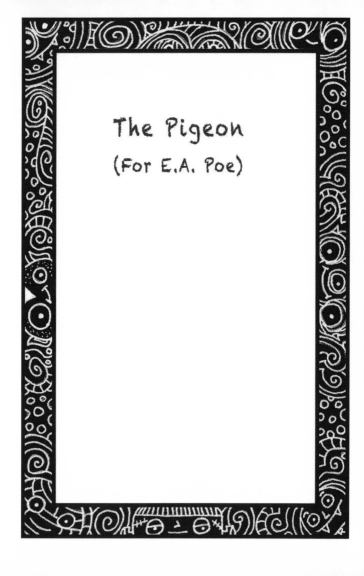

The Pigeon
(For E.A. Poe)

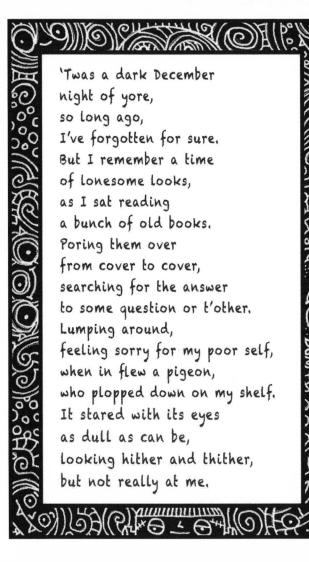

'Twas a dark December
night of yore,
so long ago,
I've forgotten for sure.
But I remember a time
of lonesome looks,
as I sat reading
a bunch of old books.
Poring them over
from cover to cover,
searching for the answer
to some question or t'other.
Lumping around,
feeling sorry for my poor self,
when in flew a pigeon,
who plopped down on my shelf.
It stared with its eyes
as dull as can be,
looking hither and thither,
but not really at me.

It seemed to know something,
this solemn old bird,
so, I asked it a question,
I know that it heard.
"Is there respite
from this sorrow and pain?
Relief for this agony
that drives me insane?
Answer me, bird,
as you perch by my door.
Will I see her again,
my lost love, Lenore?
Will I be with her now
for ever and ever more?!?"

QUOTH THE PIGEON: ...

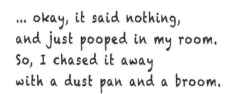

... okay, it said nothing,
and just pooped in my room.
So, I chased it away
with a dust pan and a broom.

THE END

More Books
by Jason L. Witter

Books available

on

www.amazon.com

and

www.witterworks.com

Collections of
poems & illustrations:

"The Tiniest Vampire"
(and other silly things)

"Monsters Eating Ice Cream"
(and other silly things)

"Dinosaurs at the Dentist"
(and other silly things)

CLASSICS (kind of)
Silly new adaptations of cool old stories

Bram Stoker's "Dracula"

Edgar Allan Poe's "The Raven"

Herman Melville's "Moby Dick"

Homer's "The Odyssey"

Mary Shelley's "Frankenstein"

William Shakespeare's "Hamlet"

Made in the USA
Monee, IL
05 April 2021